Christ—
the
bodybuilder

CHRIST – THE BODY BUILDER

Ian McDowall

Copyright © 2004 Ian McDowall

21 20 19 18 17 8 7 6 5 4 3 2

Reprint 2017

First published 2004 by Authentic Media, PO Box 6326,
Bletchley, Milton Keynes, MK1 9GG.

British Library Cataloguing in Publication Data
A catalogue record for this book is available from the British
Library.

9781860244780

Unless otherwise indicated, all scripture quotations are from the
New Century Version (Anglicised Edition). Copyright © 1993,
2004 by Authentic Media, PO Box 6326, Bletchley,
Milton Keynes, MK1 9GG.
All rights reserved.

Cover design by David Lund
Design and typesetting by Giles Davies Design

Printed and bound by CPI Group (UK) Ltd, Croydon, CR0 4YY

Contents

Introduction

INTRODUCTION

I did not grow up in a Christian home, as some of you will know from my story in the book Tough Talk. So when I gave my life to Christ I had many questions and fears. I had a bit of a panic attack at first. What have I done? Does this mean there's no more fun? What do I do next? Do I have to start acting like somebody else?

If anybody tells you that being a Christian is easy, they're not telling you the truth. (In fact Jesus warned us of the opposite.) I remember my brothers thinking I had gone mad, 'He's lost the plot.' But let me tell you, Jesus said, 'I came to give life – life in all its fullness.'

I can confidently say that whatever I have given up or have changed, Jesus has given me a richness and fullness of life above anything I could write or say. Where my life was dominated by fears and anxieties, now I have peace, hope and love.

However, during those early months and years I had so many questions and doubts. I don't know if it was pride or whether I was just too scared to ask. I struggled with so much of what the Church takes for granted. I remember going to church every Sunday for over two years before I really heard the gospel preached. I now understand that all these questions are perfectly normal and I have attempted in these few chapters to guide you through them.

So this is dedicated to all those who have responded in their heart to Jesus and have the sort of feelings and questions that I went through. Hey, you're normal! It's OK to have questions. And it's my privilege to have you join me in this amazing adventure of faith and life with a living God.

Keep it real

Ian McDowall

??????????????????????????

1 THE PURPOSE OF IT ALL

What is the purpose of life?

The million-dollar question. At some stage in everyone's life we come face-to-face with this question. And because there seems no real answer we try and find it in a particular interest in life. for some this could be meditation, for another religion or various hobbies. Sport often finds a way of becoming not the answer, but a temporary solution to the question. I found it in bodybuilding.

I first went to a competitive bodybuilding show when I was about sixteen. At first it seemed a strange sport: men parading around on a stage in nothing more than a pair of swimming trunks; bodies covered in baby oil. I was sitting next to an old pro and he began to explain all the ins and outs of the day's event. He pointed out how hard each man had worked-out to get his physique in such shape.

> Sport ... not the answer, but a temporary solution to the question?

He continued by explaining what the different body poses were all about, and how each competitor had to show off his body in six different rounds. Then, he told me, they went through it all again in the evening. I realised that bodybuilding was nothing like I'd imagined. All my preconceived ideas were shattered and I found myself leaving the show not only admiring the sport, but wanting to compete one day myself.

It was the same when I first encountered Christianity. I had believed that all Christians were wimps, with nothing better to do than hang around dusty church buildings, singing hymns. I was probably a God hater. I was one who asked, 'If there's a God, why is there so much pain and misery?' To me Christians seemed sad individuals who had nothing to offer. These views, I am sorry to say, are shared by the majority of the British population. Christians? Men that wear socks and sandals, women with beards and 1920s' dress sense. These are our preconceived ideas, yet how many know the Christian message, the good news, the gospel? A distant memory of a nativity play from many years ago is probably the best that can be mustered.

Yet Christianity claims to have the answer to the question. This ancient religion makes claims that need to be investigated, even today. Maybe you already consider yourself to be a Christian, or you have just made a commitment. Perhaps you're just having a little look. If you are in the first two categories then you are part of the body of Christ. Just as a bodybuilder builds his body, Christ is building his 'body', the Church, and you are part of that body: 'Together you are the body of Christ, and each one of you is a part that body' (1 Corinthians 12:27). The Church is the body and Christ is the head. The body cannot live without the head. If you remove the head, then you kill the body. When the body and the head are one, Christ comes and lives in his body by his Holy Spirit: 'And in Christ you, too, are being built together . . . into a place where God lives through the Spirit' (Ephesians 2:22).

This dwelling of God's Holy Spirit restores what is known as 'the fall of man' – you know the Adam and Eve story. 'Sin came into the world because of what one man did, and with sin came death. This is why everyone must die – because everyone sinned' (Romans 5:12). Because of what Adam did in disobeying God, he rejected God and sin entered the world. So we, by nature, are sinners. The result of Adam's sin was condemnation for all and the Bible says that the result of sin and condemnation is death – 'When people sin, they earn what sin pays – death' (Romans 6:23a).

The Bible is not a book trying to prove that God exists. No, it's a book that takes us on various journeys to show us the state of fallen humanity; how this happened; the results of this for us today; and what God has done about it (Romans 3:23 'all have sinned and are not good enough for God's glory'). We have looked for the answer to the question in many different places, but no one seeks God who has the answer (Romans 3:11). However, as I said, God has done something about it. This is the good news: 'God loved the world so much that he gave his one and only Son so that whoever believes in him may not be lost, but have eternal life' (John 3:16).

8

The Bible tells us that a curse came into effect on the day Adam disobeyed God and man 'fell' – the curse of sin and death – but that Jesus became a curse on the cross for us, to set us free from the curse of sin and death.

Jesus Christ was fully God and fully man; he was perfect in all his ways. He proved his Godly credentials by rising from the dead. Romans 1:3, 4: 'The Good News is about God's Son, Jesus Christ our Lord. As a man, he was born from the family of David. But through the Spirit of holiness he was appointed to be God's Son with great power by rising from the dead.' By believing in Jesus Christ the world can be saved: 'one good act that Christ did makes all people right with God' (Romans 5:18).

> It's not about being good, but about having faith (believing) in Jesus

So Christianity is not about bells and funny smells or weddings and funerals; it's about life's big question. It's not about being good, but about having faith (believing) in Jesus (Ephesians 2:8: 'you have been saved by grace through believing'). Acts 16:31 says, 'Believe in the Lord Jesus and you will be saved'.

What a wonderful message the Church has. Yet how will people know unless the Church, the body of Christ, tells them? That is our purpose, our driving ambition: to see that God's free gift of forgiveness and eternal life, a life of hope and destiny, a life of peace and assurance, will be accepted by all. It's more than building up numbers in our Sunday service or our youth group. It's about being lost for eternity or spending eternity with God. Jesus said to the thief who was being crucified that day with him, 'Today you will be with me in paradise'.

I have found that when the gospel is presented to the world, people are not as anti-God as you would think. On the contrary, people are searching for the real deal! In every heart there is sense of 'there's got to be more than this', a basic knowledge of right and wrong, and a conscience guiding our actions. We have a desire for our hidden secret sins to be forgiven. The world does its best to block all this out. Yet we all understand that even our dirty language is wrong – nobody wants to hear their children swearing, do they? Even our words condemn us. Yet Christ has freed us from our sins by his blood, by dying on the cross.

The world needs to hear the gospel of hope and salvation through Jesus Christ our Lord, and we are the ones he has called to tell them: our family, friends and neighbours, work colleagues and people we come into contact with.

Before I was a bodybuilder, I had no idea what the sport was all about. Then I became a competitive bodybuilder and started to see it with different eyes. People have no idea what the gospel and Christianity are all about, so Christ has left us, his body, the job of telling the good news with the help of his Holy Spirit. And, by his Holy Spirit, he will bring people into his body, and join them to him, the head.

Now, as a born-again believer, one who has decided to follow God's way, God wants you to build up his body. To build his body you need to grow and step out. The following chapters will deal with the basics of how to grow as a Christian and be effective in your faith.

NOTES FOR GROWTH

1   Pray and read God's word, asking God to help you understand his purpose for your life.

2   Ask God to help you develop in his body, the Church. He has a role for your life. You are in his plan and he has a purpose for you.

3   'We will all die some day. We're like water spilled on the ground; no one can gather it back. But God doesn't take away life. Instead, he plans ways that those who have been sent away will not have to stay away from him' (2 Samuel 14:14).

2 FINDING A GYM

At the age of fifteen I started lifting weights. My older brother, Lloyd, had bought a weightlifting set and we started pumping up in the front room. The first couple of weeks went well, then my brother changed jobs and I was left to continue on my own. Within a month it was all over – so many distractions. I would just start to train and then the TV would stop me, or the phone would ring, or somebody would come to the front door. It just wasn't happening at home; I was rapidly losing my desire to train. The weights got moved out to the conservatory and then when we had to make space they went into the cellar, never to be seen again. All my best intentions disappeared. I had all the passion in the world to start with; I was going to be the strongest in the world. I started to eat more, read the bodybuilding mags, visualise myself as a great bodybuilding champion. Yet, within a month of working-out, it was all over – like a cheap firework, showing so much potential, then fading out in a sad little whimper. Six months passed and I still had every intention of getting back into it. 'Next Monday', I would say to myself, 'I will make a fresh start'. Then another week would come and go. When Lloyd started to run his own café, he would finish work early in the afternoon, so he joined a gym: 'Wag Bennett's' – the home of East End bodybuilding.

'Ian, why not train with me at Wag's?' Lloyd suggested. And that was it! From the moment I walked into the gym and felt the atmosphere, heard the noise of the weights, saw all the different types of equipment – even the shower afterwards seemed so cool – I realised this really was for me. I remember sitting and talking to the older bodybuilders for hours, asking questions and seeking their approval. Bob was in his late forties and had a fantastic physique. He would train for hours and I would just watch. I would pick up tips, watch his style of training, copy his routine and, slowly, my own body started to develop. Before I knew it, a year had passed and I had changed so much. Training was never a chore in the gym. Growth and muscle development just kept improving. Whenever I felt like maybe it was all too much hard work, the atmosphere of the gym – all the bodybuilding talk and watching the older bodybuilders – would set the flames alight again.

How necessary is training in a gym? If you want improvement, growth or to be a champion you need to be around like-minded people: you need encouragement, instruction and a helping hand. You need to find a local gym.

Arthur White, who is a champion power-lifter and part of the Tough Talk team, often says, 'In order for me to become a world champion power-lifter, I needed to find a gym. Training at home with a ball-worker I was not going to win a world championship. I needed coaching, I needed people around me, to encourage and help me develop my strength. I was hungry, but I needed to turn that young passion into results – and I mean for the long term. I was in it for the long haul.

It's the same in my Christian life. Even though I believe it's a personal relationship between me and God, I need to be around people who will encourage me. I am in it for the long haul.'

Finding a Church

It's as important for someone in training to find a gym, as it is for somebody who has responded to the gospel message to find a church. Going to church does not make you a Christian. You can also argue that going to McDonald's doesn't make you a Big Mac – but you find Big Macs in McDonald's. Christians need to be in church: they need to be together for encouragement, for learning about their faith, for instruction and teaching. We need to develop our spiritual muscles. And for this we need people around us who think the same, who have the same belief system. We need, as Christians, to be built up in our faith, stretching and pulling our spiritual muscles.

Some people say, 'I want Jesus to forgive me of my sins, but as for church, I haven't got time for all that. I can't give any of my time for church.' Let me tell you now, Jesus gave up his whole life to build his church and demands no less from us! When we give our lives to him, that's what we mean. 'Jesus, come into my life, be the centre of all that I say and do.' God wants more than one Sunday every couple of weeks when you have nothing better on. He wants your life!

I gave my heart to Jesus in a car after a fight in a club. Some months before this, I *I began to realise that I had been living by the wrong standards in life* had prayed a prayer asking Jesus to come into my life during the night after having a dream about God. I remember waking up and telling my wife Val (who had been a Christian for many years), 'Val, I've had a terrible dream.' Sleepily she asked me about it. When I had finished she said, 'Ian, let's pray.' I remember being desperate, and praying with my wife that night just so that God would take away the bad dreams. For the next few months I wondered if that prayer could make me a Christian. Val often asked if I wanted to come to church. 'Not likely!' I remember thinking, and I would make any excuse to avoid committing myself to a visit to church.

Then it happened: the night I truly gave my heart to God. It was a normal night on the door at the nightclub. I'd been involved in a fight. I drove home; I had a gun in the boot of the car and a knife in my pocket. I remember looking down at my shirt as I drove and it was covered in blood. I remember thinking about the fight, then suddenly thinking about God. My mind was rushing backwards and forwards. I pulled into a lay-by on the A406. I had to take hold of my mind but I couldn't while I was driving. As I was sitting alone in the car, a voice, although not audible, was speaking to me. 'You've done something wrong.' I kept reasoning and arguing with myself about the incident earlier. Then, memories of other situations came into my mind. And slowly, like the breaking of day, I began to realise that I had been living by the wrong standards in life, and that before a holy God I had been out of order. The truth hit me like a sledgehammer. Not only was the violence wrong, everything I did was wrong. I felt ashamed that night, unclean and dirty. Leaning back in the car seat, I felt terrible. Never had anything evoked such emotions in me. That night I truly cried out to Jesus to forgive me and to come into my life: 'Jesus if you are real help me; come into my life, forgive me; change me Jesus.'

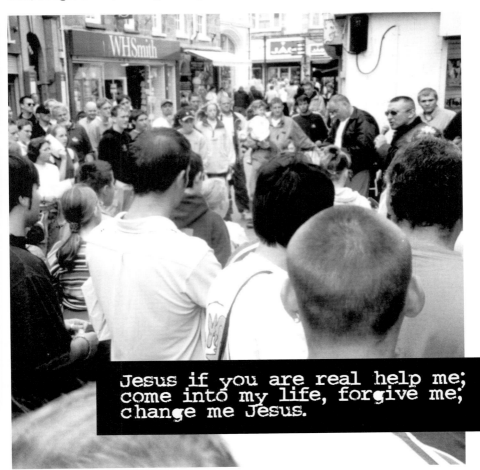

Jesus if you are real help me; come into my life, forgive me; change me Jesus.

That weekend I went to church with Val. What a difference I felt from anything before. I sat in that building listening to the preacher. I didn't understand much of his sermon, but I wept during the worship and loved the atmosphere of the place. God was real and Jesus had come into my heart.

As the months went by, Sundays couldn't come round quick enough. I couldn't get enough of worshipping and hearing about the God that had come and visited me that night. I wanted to hear how he had changed other lives, I wanted to listen to people praying and talking about him. I remember being amazed when people prayed and called him Father and seemed to really know him. I wanted more and more.

Tony was a major support to me in those early days. He was a lot like me in his background, and he had found Jesus in prison. He often invited Val and me to his house for Sunday lunch. He would encourage me and point me in the right direction when it came to praying and reading God's word. It was like watching Bob in the gym all those years ago. We need fellowship and support from other Christians.

After a while, Sunday wasn't enough; I started attending prayer evenings and a house group. I needed the support of Christians to get me through the week. I wanted my Christianity to be real. Hebrews 10:24–25 says, 'Let us think about each other and help each other to show love and do good deeds. You should not stay away from the church meetings, as some are doing, but you should meet together and encourage each other.' During my life as a Christian I have had many difficult days. Sometimes I have felt like I've been to hell and back. But help comes from the consistency of regularly spending time with other Christians. As a bodybuilder I understood that consistency in training was a key to success. In my faith, I need the prayers of my brothers and their encouragement to keep me going. 'The believers met together in the temple every day. They ate together in their homes, happy to share their food with joyful hearts. They praised God and were liked by all the people. Every day the Lord added those who were being saved to the group of believers' (Acts 2:46–47).

You need to be in a good Bible-believing church to live the li

16

You need to be in a good Bible-believing church to live the life. Something happens when you hear the word of God. Jesus explains in Mark chapter 4 that people's hearts and the word of God are like seeds and soil, let's have a look . . .

'Listen! A farmer went out to plant his seed. While he was planting, some seed fell by the road, and the birds came and ate it up. Some seed fell on rocky ground where there wasn't much earth. That seed grew very fast, because the ground was not deep. But when the sun rose, the plants dried up because they did not have deep roots. Some other seed fell among thorny weeds, which grew and choked the good plants. So those plants did not produce a crop. Some other seed fell on good ground and began to grow. It got taller and produced a crop. Some plants made 30 times more, some made 60 times more, and some made 100 times more' (Mark 4:3–8).

The seed that is sown on the path is like people who hear the word of God and immediately Satan comes and takes away that word. Some, like the seed sown on rocky places, hear the word and believe, but they don't make any roots, so they last only a short time. When difficult times come they quickly give up. Seed sown among thorns is like people who hear and accept the good news of God, yet worries of this life, the deceitfulness of wealth, and the desires for other things come in and choke the word, making it unfruitful. Seed sown in good soil is like people who hear the word, accept it and put down roots and go on to grow and produce a crop.

Take a moment and notice the first two types of people who fall away. The first falls immediately, so the chances are, you, the reader, are in one of the other three categories. Those sown in rocky places are doomed to fall away in times of pressure: they believe gladly, yet fall away when they face difficulties in life.

Before we get to the 'good soil', notice that those which grow among 'thorns' do not fall away, but their Christian life seems unbearable. They have worries, they desire things, and they have deceitful hearts. They never truly make Jesus Lord of their lives; they are looking back towards the things of the world, pursuing wealth and not him. How many are in church each week, yet instead of being free in Christ they are still locked in to sin? They have a 'religion', but lack the freedom of a trusting relationship with God. They attend church out of duty. There is belief and unbelief. (Mark 9:24 'Immediately the boy's father exclaimed, "I do believe; help me overcome my unbelief!"') They do the church thing, but if they never get to know Jesus as Lord they may one day hear his voice say, 'Get away from me you who do evil. I never knew you' (Matthew 7:23). Strong words, but they come directly from Jesus. Get right with God the Father and make Jesus boss of your life. If you know this is how you feel pray this prayer right now:

'Father, I know only you know the motives of my heart, and I feel bound and worn out pursuing the things in this life. But by the power of your Holy Spirit I ask, Father, that you would set me free. I want to make you truly in charge of my life, of my thoughts and actions. I ask this in the name of Jesus.

Amen.'

Joining a church is vital for your growth. You will find support, friendship and people who will pray for you. You will be part of the body of Christ. If you are not in a church, pray and find yourself a church. Living the Christian life is a fight of faith. The devil wants to cloud your thinking, knock what you believe and cause you to doubt. Notice that the good soil produces fruit. God wants you to be fruitful: in your life; having relationships that last; to be fruitful in sharing your faith; fruitful in your work and in your marriage; fruitful in every aspect of your life. This will only be possible if you meet together with others. Do not let anything stop you from finding a church – it's the only way to develop your spiritual muscles and build your faith.

NOTES FOR GROWTH

1   Find a good Bible-believing church – a church that worships the Lord Jesus Christ and teaches from the Bible. Look for a church that has activities during the week, cell groups or house groups. Churches that run Alpha courses are a good guideline.

2   A bodybuilder needs a balanced physique. He must develop his legs as well as his arms. A Christian needs a balance to his walk. To enable you to achieve this you need relationships with other Christians, giving you support, encouragement and teaching. You will need the help of others, as you walk your walk of faith.

3   'And let us consider how we may spur one another on towards love and good deeds. Let us not give up meeting together, as some are in the habit of doing; let us encourage one another' (Hebrews 10:24).

3 PRAYER AND WORKING OUT

'When you pray, don't be like the hypocrites. They love to stand in the synagogues and on the street corners and pray so that people will see them. I tell you the truth, they already have their full reward. When you pray, you should go into your room and close the door and pray to your Father who cannot be seen. Your Father can see what is done in secret, and he will reward you. And when you pray, don't be like those people who don't know God. They continue saying things that mean nothing, thinking that God will hear them because of their many words. Don't be like them, because your Father knows the things you need before you ask him. So when you pray, you should pray like this:

"Our Father in heaven,
    may your name always be
                    kept holy.

May your kingdom come,
and what you want be done,
here on earth as it is in
heaven.

    Give us the food we need for
                    each day.

Forgive us for our sins,
just as we have forgiven
those who sinned against us.

    And do not cause us to be
    tempted, but save us from
                the Evil One.

(Matthew 6:5–13)

21

The starting point of bodybuilding is training. Trying to build up your body without working-out will never work: no matter how much you eat, you will just get fat. The starting point for faith in Christ is prayer: you talk to him and respond to him by prayer. To become a Christian you have to pray. It may be as simple as saying to him in your head, 'Jesus I need you,' but that is your starting point. Prayer is your direct route to a relationship with your heavenly Father. Your spirit has been born again and it needs to be developed. When you first enter a gym, especially a bodybuilding gym, you feel out of place, lost! Like a child entering an unknown world. This will be the same for you when you start your prayer life for the first time. As you begin exercising for the first time you feel uncomfortable; the atmosphere is not what you are used to. Is anyone looking at me? Have I got the right kit on? Am I doing this right? Is this really going to work? It seems so hard and my technique doesn't feel right. Where's the instructor? Somebody help! Somebody get me out of here! This training thing is not for me!

> Prayer is your direct route to a relationship with your heavenly Father

You are now ready to develop your spiritual muscles, but before you start flexing you have to start developing. Entering your prayer room for the first time is just like entering the gym for the first time. Jesus said that when you pray you should go into your room, close the door, and pray to your Father who is unseen. This is where your relationship with God begins. It's you and him, and he is unseen. This is the uncomfortable bit; this is the part when you first feel out of place. The first time you do anything you feel out of place. When going to a gym for the first time you feel so uncomfortable. It is the same when you go into your room on your own to pray. You start by praying to an unseen God. You see yourself out of place. It's not your thing. The thoughts and suggestions start to attack your mind: 'Look at me. I've been an unbeliever all my life, now I'm closing my eyes and praying. It was OK at that meeting when the guy prayed for me, but now I don't think so! Forget praying out loud when I'm the only one in the room. I can never be a Christian. Who am I kidding? Let me put an end to it now; let me stop this. I don't need a crutch to lean on, never have before, so why now? Let me put a stop to this before it's too late! It was easier before.'

Entering that prayer room is like entering church for the first time: everything seems to tell you to stop, pray at church but not in your bedroom; pray with others but not on your own. Let me

tell you, your personal walk and relationship with God depends on you getting to know him personally. And it starts by going into the room and closing your door. Jesus said that you 'pray to your Father who is unseen,' and then he says, 'your Father who sees'. You may not see Jesus, but he sees you. How can this be? How come God can see me but I can't see him? How can he hear me or see me? Stop trying to work it all out in your head. The Bible says God's eyes are on the righteous and his ears are attentive to their prayers. When I use my mobile phone, I press the green button and, before I know it, I'm talking to my wife, Val. When I close my eyes and, by faith, I talk to God, by faith I know he hears me. His Holy Spirit somehow takes my prayers into his presence. The book of Revelation says in chapter 8 verse 4 that the prayers of God's people are like incense – in other words, like a fragrance that comes before God's presence. Yes, he hears you before you pray and he knows what you want and, yes, he can hear you even if you don't talk out loud. But you need to demonstrate your faith and let his Holy Spirit not only take your prayers to God but also help you pray. Let the relationship begin.

How to start?

How do I start? Start by addressing him, like having a telephone conversation: 'Our Father in heaven, may your name always be kept holy.' Not only is he your Father but he is also God. And his name is holy. Have fear and respect for him as God. If you ever stand and look at the power of the elements or the awesome power of the sea, or your breath is taken by the view from a mountain, then how much more awesome is the God who created all these things? 'Through his power all things were made – things in heaven and on earth' (Colossians 1:16).

Have fear (or respect) for him as God, your creator. The Bible says that fear of God is the beginning of wisdom. Yet Jesus says we are to call him Father. The word 'father' will have different meanings to different people. I never knew my earthly father. An absent father can bring feelings of abandonment, maybe rejection. A violent father brings feelings of fear and hatred. Some fathers just ignore their children, showing neither love nor dislike. I had the love of a mother, but a father can bring a different love. The apostle Paul, talking about how he treated the church in Thessalonica says, 'But we were very gentle with you, like a mother caring for her little children. Because we loved you . . . ' (1 Thessalonians 2:7). He continues in verses 11 and 12, showing how a father loves and brings a different balance, 'You know that we treated each of you as a father treats his own children. We encouraged you, we told you and we insisted that you lived good lives for God'. A father should bring love and encouragement, giving a child security, a sense of purpose and character.

Whatever a father means to you, your heavenly Father is approachable; he will never leave you or forsake you. You can put your trust in him and he will never disappoint you. He may discipline you for your own good, but this is because you are his

24

and he is your Father. Hebrews 12:7 says, 'God is treating you as children. All children are disciplined by their fathers? If you are never disciplined . . . you are not true children.' It goes on in verse 11, 'We do not enjoy being disciplined. It is painful, but later, after we have learned from it, we have peace, because we start living in the right way.' He wants you to develop in your faith, to build backbone and character so that you may share his life with others.

Unlike the father who does not take notice, your heavenly Father knows what you need. Jesus said, 'Don't worry and say, "What will we eat?" or "What will we drink?" or "What will we wear?" The people who don't know God keep trying to get these things, and your Father in heaven knows that you need them. The thing you should want most is God's kingdom and doing what God wants. Then all these other things you need will be given to you' (Matthew 6:31–33).

As a child I didn't have a father to ask anything from. Then my mother remarried and for some years I had a stepfather. Because I wasn't his son I never felt comfortable asking him for anything, as if it wasn't really my right. I felt he was unapproachable, and if I should get something from him then I should feel grateful. In truth, this man helped to put a roof over my head, clothe and feed me. Yet for me there always seemed to be a barrier there. As Christians we often come to God our Father with the same attitude: why should God answer my prayer? There are so many problems in the world, why would he be interested in me? He seems unapproachable and we feel almost guilty for asking anything from him. However, Jesus says in Matthew 7:7–8, 'Ask, and God will give to you. Search and you will find. Knock and the door will open for you. Yes, *everyone* who asks will receive. Everyone who searches will find. And everyone who knocks will have the door opened' (my emphasis). Jesus is showing us that our heavenly Father wants us to come to him and ask him; to bring our problems, our financial needs, family issues, our emotions and thoughts to him. Jesus continues in 7:9–11, 'If your children ask for bread, which of you would give them a stone? Or if your children ask for a fish, would you give them a snake? Even though you are bad, you know how to give good gifts to your children. How much more will your heavenly Father give good things to those who ask him!' Notice how Jesus concludes with 'those who ask him'. You must build up your relationship with God, talk to him, ask him, do not feel your requests are not important to him. Yes, he knows your needs, but he wants to hear from you. By faith call out to him. 'Do not worry about anything, but pray and ask God for everything you need, always giving thanks' (Philippians 4:6).

he knows your needs, but he wants to hear from you

One day Jesus was walking through Jericho and a crowd had gathered. As he was leaving the city, a blind man was sitting by the roadside begging. When the man heard who was walking by he started to shout, 'Jesus, Son of David, have mercy on me!' Jesus asked the man, 'What do you want me to do for you?' (Mark 10:51). Surely it must have been obvious to Jesus what the man wanted. The man was blind, he had to beg because of his blindness. He's the Son of God, he's the one that knows men's thoughts, and yet he asks the man, 'What do you want me to do for you?'

He wants our prayer requests; he wants us to ask him! Call out to your heavenly Father with your requests and see the hand of the living God deal with the impossible. After giving my heart to God, I would pray for the ability to 'walk the walk', for him to take away the depression in my life, the feelings of rejection, the bitterness and anger. I found that as I asked him he would be there for me. Working from the inside out, he gave me new direction, a reason to live, and my relationship with him began.

We are serving a living God. There is no such thing as a step-by-step 'this is how to pray' or 'this is how to get your prayers answered'. Every day he wants you to gain a better understanding of him and you. As you get to know him, you will start to see yourself for who you really are with all your strengths but, even more, your weaknesses! The Christian walk must always be a balanced walk. Never think that because you have found a scripture that says 'ask and you will receive' that this means for one moment that no matter what your requests are God will answer and give you anything. This is not what is being taught here. You need balance and maturity; he wants to build a relationship with you, he wants to use you to serve his kingdom. (James 4:2–3: 'You do not get what you want, because you do not ask God. Or when you ask, you do not receive because the reason you ask is wrong. You want things so you can use them for your own pleasures.')

However, be assured, he wants your requests, he wants to walk with you, to be your God.

NOTES FOR GROWTH:

1   Your relationship begins in your personal prayer room.

2   Always pray to God the Father in the name of Jesus.

3   Jesus wants you to ask him.

4   'You do not get what you want because you do not ask God. Or when you ask you do not receive because the reason you ask is wrong. You want things so you can use them for your own pleasures' (James 4:2b).

5   'When a believing person prays, great things happen' (James 5:16b).

4 FLEXING YOUR SPIRITUAL MUSCLES

'Forgive us for our sins, just as we have forgiven those who sinned against us. And do not cause us to be tempted, but save us from the Evil One' (Matthew 6:12,13).

We started the previous chapter with what is known as the 'Lord's Prayer', which was the prayer model Jesus used to teach his disciples how to pray. In Matthew 6:9 Jesus tells us how to approach our Father in heaven – with reverence for his name – and that we should want to see his kingdom come. I often thank God when I pray for all that he has done for me on the cross. Don't forget this is your personal time with him, for getting to know him. As a 'baby' Christian and you may only pray for a couple of minutes. However, as you mature spiritually and your faith grows and your relationship with him grows, you will begin to develop your spiritual muscles and the time spent alone with him will grow.

When you start to train, the first session in the gym may only last twenty minutes, you will probably be sore for a few days and, therefore, you may only train once or twice a week. However, the fitter you are the more exercise your body will need to stimulate growth. This principle will also be evident in your walk with God. Your spirit, the part of you that grows within, the part inside that communicates with God, will want more. The Bible says that your spirit needs to be filled with his Holy Spirit and that your spirit and your flesh (sinful nature) are in conflict with each other. There is a war going on within you. Romans 8:13 says, 'If you use your lives to do the wrong things your sinful selves want, you will die spiritually. But if you use the Spirit's help to stop doing the wrong things you do with your body, you will have true life.'

Two dogs

Putting all this simply, I had a friend who I had known for many years. He grew up in a typical East End family and, as a young man, got involved in all sorts of crime and drug taking. Then he came to know Jesus Christ. However, he constantly wrestled with things from his past, and found it all a massive struggle.

We were talking one day and he said, 'Ian, I feel like there are two dogs fighting within me, like a battle going on.'
'So which dog is going to win?' I asked.
He thought for a moment and said, 'The one that gets fed the most.'

Simple stuff – feed your spirit with prayer. Develop those spiritual muscles and see how you grow. You will overcome those weaknesses, habits and addictions as you offer yourself to God. From seeing his kingdom come, he wants us to bring our daily needs to him: 'Give us the food we need for each day'. Then we look at our heart. It says in Matthew 6:12, (in the Contemporary English Version), 'forgive us for doing wrong as we forgive others.' Jesus, at this point, asks us to look within ourselves. This can become a very uncomfortable thing. When you look at yourself with God's eyes, you will see things inside you wish you had never seen.

> God lovingly began to show me the real inside: arrogance, pride, selfish ambition and unforgiveness

I remember training as a bodybuilder for a couple years and then deciding to compete. I thought, as I stood a couple of feet away from a mirror, 'Yeah, you're in good shape.' I stood there flexing my muscles thinking, 'A little more size maybe, but not bad.' Then I gave it a go. I went out on stage for the first time, with nothing more than swimming trunks (we called them posing briefs) on. I stood there in front of hundreds of people, doing muscle poses, thinking I looked fantastic. Then when I realised I hadn't made the top three I couldn't believe it. 'I've been robbed!' I thought. So I bought the video. Then it became plainly evident. I was actually terrible. I had not built or developed my body to anywhere near the size I thought it was. It was like looking at myself for the first time. And it wasn't pretty.

As a Christian, it felt the same when God lovingly began to show me the real inside: arrogance, pride, selfish ambitions and unforgiveness. Unforgiveness is a serious business. So much so that God reiterates this point a few moments later in Matthew 6:14–15 (CEV): 'If you forgive others for the wrongs they have done you, your Father in heaven will forgive you. But if you do not forgive others, your Father will not forgive you.'

You may say to me, 'Ian, I can't forgive her or him, you don't know what they've done to me.' I have spoken to people in prison who have been through hell and back; abused sexually, physically and mentally. And I have had to look them in the eye and say, 'I know that I don't understand what they have done or what you have been through. However, I know that you must forgive them, and then your Father in heaven will forgive you. I know that you can't do it on your own, but if you ask God to help you forgive it is possible.'

If you know here and now as you read this that you have unforgiveness within you then start to flex your spiritual muscles and sow the seed of forgiveness. Right now, say:

'**Father** I know that I have said so many times that I can't forgive her or him for what they have done to me, but right now I pray and say I forgive them, **as you have forgiven me.** I pray this in the name of Jesus.'

Forgiveness is a key to your freedom, your freedom to worship, witness and walk with Jesus

Pumping up

At last you have started, you're moving the cables, pushing the bar and you're beginning to feel like you belong in this gym after all. Yes, all feels good, you can see your shape improving, and you're beginning to understand some of the gym jargon. You're feeling like you belong. You're pumping up!

As you walk down the street you're feeling good. You've had your shower and you feel alive, fresh and fit. You have just done a 45-minute workout and you can conquer anything. Nothing is going to stop you now!

Oh boy, then it happens. You turn the corner and suddenly you smell it. Mmmmm. What is that? It smells lovely. Then your eyes lock on and fix in. It's the local bakery and, man, does something smell good today. You say to yourself, 'Just a little look in the window, why that won't hurt. It's not like I'm eating any of that junk food. Just a little look.' You stand there looking through the window, and realise at the same moment as your eyes see your favourite cake, 'Wow, I feel so hungry!' Standing there you find yourself licking your lips. 'My, the cream looks good.' Then you try to pull yourself together; shaking your shoulders you pull your head away. 'What's wrong with me? It's the last thing I need after all that work. Just keep walking.' Your legs begin to move and you pass the door. And you think you've made it. Then it happens . . . the second window. The pastry section, and does it smell and look good. You find an irresistible pull back towards the shop. The next thing you know, there you are at the counter. 'Just one cake,' you say to yourself, 'one won't harm me.' As you're thinking this, suddenly you find your mouth out of control. Two sausage rolls and a couple of those cream and jam doughnuts. Was that me or somebody behind me? But, low and behold, within minutes you're walking down the street shovelling 2,000 calories of junk food down you, like a man out of control. And then, just as you're licking your fingers, as the final bit of jam is on your tongue, you feel it. 'What's wrong with me? All that work! Do I have no control? What have I done?'

Jesus said, 'do not cause us to be tempted, but save us from the Evil One' (Matthew 6:13). This is how it happens. We can walk out of that prayer meeting, church service or conference feeling on top of the world, 'Wow, my God is with me. Nothing can stop me now! Man, I can walk on water, just show me those mountains now baby! We'll see who's got faith.' Then it happens: you bump into that old flame, the betting shop or your favourite pub. It could be a drug dealer, a dirty mag, the good old boys or the good

32

old girls. Your temptations will always be different to those of somebody else. Your problem, your temper will be unique to you. 'But if you do not do what is right, sin is crouching at your door; it desires to have you, but you must master it' (Genesis 4:7b, NIV). The devil knows how to get you going, and he knows what it will take to make you feel condemned. It tastes and smells good. And everything inside says you want it, you must have it, just one more won't harm. But, boy, in your heart you know different, something's telling you to move on, keep going, don't look back. But how can you resist? It just seems like an irresistible pull towards the thing you don't want to do. The apostle Paul said it like this in Romans 7:15, 'I do not do what I want to do, I do the things I hate' and again in 7:19, 'I do not do the good things I want to do, but I do the bad things I do not want to do.'

Temptation, a seductive force

Proverbs takes us on a journey showing us how temptation can bring us down. We pick up the story at chapter 7 verse 7: 'I saw some foolish young men. I noticed one of them had no wisdom. He was walking down the street near the corner, on the road leading to her house. It was the twilight of the evening, as the darkness of the night was beginning. Then the woman approached him, dressed like a prostitute and planning to trick him. She was loud and stubborn and never stayed at home. She was always in the streets or in the city squares, waiting around on the corners of the streets. She took hold of him and kissed him. Without shame she said to him: "I made my fellowship offerings and took some of the meat home. Today I have kept my special promises. So I have come out to meet you; I have been looking for you and have found you. I have covered my bed with coloured sheets from Egypt. I have made my bed smell sweet with myrrh, aloes and cinnamon. Come, let's make love until morning. Let's enjoy each other's love. My husband is not home; he has gone on a long trip.'"

Let's take a quick look at what we have read, and break it down for our ammunition. Notice how the young man is walking in her direction. Always take care of your thoughts; never let them wander down towards the path of sin. Keep a hold of your thinking; the Bible says to take captive every thought and make it obedient to Christ. Jesus said that we should pray 'lead us away from temptation' or 'do not cause us to be tempted'. Notice the phrase, 'Then the woman approached him'. Temptation will come out in an effort to take hold of you. Even at this stage you still have the ability to resist. The Bible says, 'Stand against the devil, and the devil will run from you' (James 4:7).

Every Christian will face temptations. Jesus faced temptations in the desert on our behalf. It's a weapon of the devil, for when sin is fully-grown, when it goes from thought to action, it leads to death (and unbelief). We are assured in 1 Corinthians 10:13 that God will provide a way out. If you want him more than the sin, call out to him and he will give you the strength to say no, to walk away. 'The only temptation that has come to you is that which everyone has. But you can trust God; who will not let you be tempted more than you can stand. But when you are tempted, he will also give you a way to escape so that you will be able to stand it.'

At this point in our story, the temptress has kissed him and seduced him with her persuasive words. Let's return to the story at verse 21: 'by her pleasing words she led him into doing wrong. All at once he followed her, like an ox led to the butcher.' Like an ox led to the butcher – think of how powerful an ox is, strong and full of life. Just like the young man, full of testosterone and life. Just how we feel when we've been pumped up at some meeting, or conference. Be on your guard when you're feeling confident, for God wants you to feel confident only in him.

34

Self-confidence will lead you to temptation. Often, when you have just been blessed and you're on top of a mountain, you're feeling spiritually strong, that's the time to be on your guard. Ask God to lead you away from temptation.

The Old Testament is full of stories of heroes doing exploits in the name of God, then the next moment fleeing in fear of the devil or being tempted and seduced, like Samson with Delilah. Another classic is Elijah on mount Carmel. Elijah, one of God's prophets, takes on all the prophets of Baal (a false god). In 1 Kings chapter 18 our hero is making a challenge to the prophets of Baal in front of the people of Israel. 1 Kings 18:21: 'If the Lord is the true God, follow him, but if Baal is the true God, follow him!' He cries out to the people, but they say nothing. So he makes a challenge to see whose god is the living God, and whose will answer prayer. Elijah spends the next fifteen verses taunting the prophets of Baal as they pray and fail to get a response. Then Elijah prays (verse 37): 'Lord, answer my prayer so these people will know that you, Lord, are God and that you will change their minds.' The living God answered Elijah's prayers and demonstrated his power and the people fell prostrate and cried, 'The Lord is God! The Lord is God!'(verse 39).

After such a triumph, we find our hero in chapter 19 fleeing from a witch named Jezebel. 'He was afraid and ran for his life' (19:3). Never think you can do anything in your own strength. You must find your strength in God.

When an athlete trains, it's when he is at his strongest that he is at the greatest risk of an injury. Pushing heavier than ever before, running a second faster than before. Be on your guard. Proverbs 7:22–27: 'like a deer caught in a trap and shot through the liver with an arrow. Like a bird caught in a trap, he didn't know what he did would kill him. Now, my sons, listen to me; pay attention to what I say. Don't let yourself be tricked by such a woman; don't go where she leads you. She has ruined many good men, and many have died because of her. Her house is on the road to death, the road that leads down to the grave.'

Remember, the consequence of sin is death but, as Christians, we have been saved by grace. When we fall into sin, the Bible says in 1 John 1:9, 'If we confess our sins, he will forgive our sins, because we can trust God to do what is right.' Yet God has called us out of sin and wants to keep us from it and its temptations. Romans 1:5 says that we have been called out of sin 'to believe and obey'. The devil wants to get us back into sin and then, ultimately, unbelief. But our heavenly Father wants the best for us, and he wants us to walk with him. But he wants us to ask for help to keep us from temptation, and to deliver us from the evil one.

NOTES FOR GROWTH

1   When you're in your prayer room, as well as asking for your needs, ask for his divine protection and to be kept from temptation.

2   Bring your requests to your heavenly Father and ask!

3   Begin to develop your spiritual muscles with personal prayer. Jesus said, in Matthew 5:14, 'You are the light that gives light to the world,' and in verse 16, 'In the same way, you should be a light for other people. Live so that they will see the good things you do and will praise your Father in heaven'.

4   Fight the good fight of faith. Our battle is against spiritual forces. Forces that bring temptations, which lead to sin and unbelief.

5   'So give yourselves completely to God. Stand against the devil and the devil will run from you. Come near to God and God will come near to you' (James 4:7–8).

5 FOOD: THE ONLY WAY TO GROW

'Jesus answered, "It is written in the Scriptures, 'A person does not live by eating only bread, but by everything God says'"' (Matthew 4:4).

As a young man, I spent hours in the gym without any return. No matter how many times I trained, my body wasn't growing. I tried heavy weights, light weights, slow movement and fast, supersets and pyramids. Yet nothing seemed to work. Then, one day, I poured out my problems to the gym owner, Wag.
'The problem, son, is that you need to eat.'
'I do, Wag,' I responded.
'No, I mean really eat – food that will make you grow. Look, son,' he continued, 'when you're a child you need food to help you grow and to keep you alive. When you grow older you need food to maintain your health and to keep you alive; a balanced diet is what you need. But as a bodybuilder, you need to eat to grow. More calories, more proteins: milk, eggs and meats. More carbs: cereals, pasta and potatoes. Fats, vitamins, minerals. If you want to grow, Ian, you need to eat.'

So eat I did. Sometimes I felt like I was eating all day long. But I started to grow, so I ate and ate more. My bodyweight went from 12 stone to 13, 14, 15, 16, 17 stone within eighteen months. I was eating so much, all I did was cook and prepare food and eat. At one stage I remember my jaw actually locked. It was as if a clamp had suddenly attached itself to my jaw and it would neither open nor shut. Yet the moment I could move it again I carried on eating.

I remember winning a bodybuilding contest and a local paper wanted to do an article about me. So they took my photo and interviewed me, and we talked about how much I was eating. I told them that I was eating probably fifteen eggs a day. I would eat them scrambled; I would eat them poached; I would eat them blended with milk. They calculated that I had been eating at least 5,460 a year, so the article read, 'Eggstra strong Ian eats 5,460 eggs a year'. Not exactly the headline I was hoping for!

And so I went on eating and eating. However, as I got closer to competing, I found it was not just the quantity but also the quality of the food that was important. Food was at the very heart of my training. I spent the whole day preparing it, writing down every detail of what I was eating. I knew how to eat to put on weight; I knew how to eat to reduce body fat; I knew what to eat for energy; the difference between simple carbs and complex carbs, and the effect all this had on my body.

Food for a Christian is the written word of God – the Bible.

You need to eat and digest it to grow. But how do you start? You wouldn't feed a

newborn baby a roast beef dinner; you'd start by feeding them milk. In the same way, a baby Christian needs milk, not solid food. Therefore, do not treat the Bible as any other book. If you do you will struggle through Genesis, keep falling asleep through the pages of Exodus, and then you will be scratching your head with questions such as: What is the Ephod? and What is the consecration of the priest all about?

And then you come to Leviticus and you find yourself drifting between the burnt offering and the sin offering. What are all these strange regulations and laws all about? Rules for priests and unacceptable sacrifices, punishments and rewards – what's going on? Then there's Numbers and Deuteronomy, and if it's the first time you've read the Bible it's like getting lost in a forest at night.

So where is a good place to start? Take a journey through the Gospels – Matthew, Mark, Luke and John – which tell of the life of Jesus. Take extra time as you read John chapter 3 and Matthew chapters 5 to 7. Be encouraged and challenged by God's word. Study the accounts of the crucifixion and see how the attitudes of the disciples changed from the upper room to Gethsemane, the promises they made and then how they all deserted Jesus during his arrest and trials. Then consider how he forgave them at the resurrection, but how some still doubted until they saw him face-to-face. Notice, also, how they all seemed to be in hiding until Acts chapter 2 records the amazing transformation at Pentecost. Continue in Acts with the birth of the Church and how the first Christians lived and proclaimed the good news, even facing death themselves for the sake of the kingdom.

Let these men and women be your guide and goal: no longer conforming to the ways of the world, but living to God's standards. 'God's word is alive and working and is sharper than a double-edged sword. It cuts all the way into us, where the soul and the spirit are joined, to the centre of our joints and bones. And it judges the thoughts and feelings in our hearts. Nothing in all the world can be hidden from God' (Hebrews 4:12–13). Jesus makes a remarkable statement: 'A person does not live by eating only bread alone, but by everything the Lord says' (Numbers 8:3). And again he says, in John 6:51, 'I am the living bread that came down from heaven. Anyone who eats this bread will live for ever.'

The written word of God becomes a life source to our spirits

The Bible is the written word of God and the born-again believer must read God's word with the help of the Holy Spirit or he will die spiritually. Reading the word of God is good, but we need the Holy Spirit when reading to help us and to bring life to it. And this life is in Jesus. Jesus is also referred to as 'the Word': 'In the beginning there was the Word. The Word was with God, and the Word was God' (John 1:1.). And again in John 1:14: 'The Word became human and lived among us.' So we as Christians believe that the Bible is more than just a book; we believe that all Scripture was given by God. 2 Timothy 3:16 says, 'All Scripture is given by God and is useful for teaching . . . .' The written word of God becomes a life source to our spirits. We're nourished by it. We use it to teach us new ways of thinking. We spend time thinking about it (Psalm 1:2, 'They love the Lord's teachings, and they think about those teachings day and night'). We keep it in our hearts (Romans 10:8, 'The word is near you; it is in your mouth and in your heart'). We digest his word so that when we pray, or share our faith, the Holy Spirit brings his word alive.

When we eat our food it keeps us alive, and when we are putting on weight, as a child or like a bodybuilder, we eat to grow. So, likewise, our spiritual body needs spiritual food to keep us alive. In John 6:58 Jesus says, 'I am the bread that came down from heaven, and whoever eats this bread will live for ever'. Jesus is that bread, so we must feed on him and his word, the Bible, in order to live as Christians. The bodybuilder eats and grows on the outside, and you can see with your eyes how big he becomes. The body-weight increases, his muscles get bigger and it is obvious to all that he has grown. As I said, my bodyweight kept increasing the more I ate. Likewise, our spiritual body needs to grow and develop; we need to move from milk to solid food, so that our faith increases. Faith grows from hearing and reading the word of God.

Christians need to eat God's word, digest it and then regurgitate it, for when we talk, sing, laugh

40

or cry our spirit is being displayed. That's why Jesus said, 'It is not what people put into their mouths that makes them unclean. It is what comes out of their mouths that makes them unclean' (Matthew 15:11). When you listen to somebody, you can tell a lot about what's going on inside by what they say: their insecurities, fears, anxieties, unforgiveness, bitterness. Our mouths condemn us and show the world what we are really like: fault-finding, grumbling and self-seeking. 'I just want to start living for myself,' 'me, me, me – always looking after number one'. That's why Jesus says in Matthew 7:2, 'You will be judged in the same way that you judge others, and the amount you give to others will be given to you.' And again, in 12:34–37, 'The mouth speaks the things that are in the heart. Good people have good things in their hearts, and so they say good things. But evil people have evil in their hearts, so they say evil things. And I tell you that on the Judgement Day people will be responsible for every careless

thing they have said. The words you have said will be used to judge you. Some of your words will prove you right, but some of your words will prove you guilty.'

Notice Jesus says we will speak what is stored up in our hearts. That is why we must store up his words in our hearts. We must fill our hearts and minds with the word of God. This builds up our spiritual bodies and our spiritual muscles. Allow God's word to become part of your life, meditate upon it, study it and fall in love with it. Build yourself up on milk and then move on to more solid food, so that when Judgement Day comes you will be able to stand blameless.

And we at Tough Talk pray that the Bible will be like a lamp for your feet and a light for your path.

NOTES FOR GROWTH

1   A bodybuilder needs food to grow, a Christian needs God's word for spiritual growth. Food is needed every day – three meals a day is a basic requirement. Likewise, a Christian needs the nourishment of God's word every day.

2   Have a Bible by your bed, have a quick read at night then in the morning. Keep one at work. Make an effort to read something every day.

3   If time is short, read a few Proverbs or Psalms. If you have longer, read a letter from the New Testament.

4   'A person does not live on bread alone, but by everything God says' (Mathew 4:4).

6 THIS IS WHAT LIFE WAS ALL ABOUT FOR ME!

Jesus said to his followers, 'Go everywhere in the world, and tell the Good News to everyone.'

'Ladies and Gentlemen, the European and World Heavyweight Champion of 1992, from Great Britain, Arthur White.'

The applause was deafening. Walking towards the rostrum with the sound of the crowd in my ears, I felt myself swelling up, ready to burst. As I drew alongside the MC, out of the corner of my mouth, I said to him: 'Would yer say that again?'

'Ladies and Gentlemen, the . . . '

His words puffed me up even more. By the time I reached the rostrum I felt I had added ten feet to my six-foot frame. This was what life was all about for me – winning, coming first.

Swaggering across the platform, I raised my hand to acknowledge my followers who were still clapping. Up on the rostrum the applause sounded like thunder. I lifted my hands and turned from side to side. Flashes of light from photographers and the bright light from TV cameras boosted my ego again. This was the 'ultimate' for me: the pinnacle of my sixteen years as an international athlete. I bent my head to receive the medal that Keiron Stanley, President of the British Power-lifting Organisation, placed over my head. In fact, that evening I picked up no less than five medals: European Champion, European Best Lifter, World Champion, Runner-up World Best Lifter and British Power-lifting Hall of Fame.

This was what life was all about for me!
Tough Talk – Arthur White

Within each of us is a need to have direction and purpose, to feel that our life has a meaning – some sort of goal. Not many of us are like Arthur who actually achieved his ambitions. We have a vacuum inside us that can only be filled by fulfilling God's call on our lives. Even as Christians, we often feel that life has somehow let us down. We have our midlife crisis, we move house, change jobs and take holidays. But nothing can satisfy this feeling. Some people drink more, work harder or even try to run a marathon – but only doing God's will can satisfy.

Things achieved in our daily pursuits outside Christ will never satisfy this hole. You may reach your target, get your promotion, take early retirement, finish your studies, but you will be left feeling somehow not quite satisfied.

Arthur achieved all that he had set out to achieve, winning every competition that he entered, becoming World Champion, yet that very same evening, after achieving so much, Arthur felt the intense pain of an empty life. All that success, and yet this World Champion power-lifter found himself wanting to commit suicide. Arthur recalls in the book *Tough Talk*:

'The curtains were drawn, and the side lamp cast an eerie glow which matched my mood. The coke and booze had

worn off. The mask that I had upheld throughout the day was gone. This was the real me. The nightmare that I was living had now come home to haunt me. Sitting in the armchair, I held my head in my hands and wept. This should have been a time of celebration. My wife and kids should have been with me, sharing in my victory. Instead, I was a broken mess. My hard, steel-like exterior was one great big lie? I was a lonely man. . . . Tears streamed down my eyes, blinding my vision. The pain of my sobbing was cutting into every part of me. My chest felt sore with all the heaving and deep emotion that I was experiencing. Now would be the time, I thought, to end it all.'

In Jesus there is a fullness of life. Jesus said 'I came to give life – life in all its fullness' (John 10:10). You have been saved by grace. However, the Bible says that he has done this so you can do good works. Ephesians 2:8–10: 'I mean that you have been saved by grace through believing. You did not save yourselves: it was a gift from God. It was not the result of your own work, so you cannot boast about it. God has made us what we are. In Christ Jesus, God made us to do good works, which God planned in advance for us to live our lives doing.'

God has a plan for your life

The hole inside that drives us towards making our lives count can only be satisfied in Jesus Christ. Once the initial excitement of becoming World Champion had faded, Arthur was left with a great emptiness. And as we grow older, life's constant disappointments create a huge void. All those regrets and unfulfilled dreams add up, leaving us feeling numb and unimportant. But the God who said, 'Let us make human beings in our image and likeness. And let them rule the fish in the sea and the birds in the sky, over the tame animals, over all the earth, and over all the small crawling animals on the earth' (Genesis 1:26) has a plan for your life. He has made you to do good works, to make a difference in a decaying world.

Our God of creation, the one who formed the universe, has a plan for your life. 2 Samuel 14:14 says, 'We will all die some day. We're like water spilled on the ground; no one can gather it back. But God doesn't take away life. Instead, he plans ways that those that have been sent away will not have to stay away from him!' God has worked out a plan for you. He has planned work for you to do. And at the top of the plan is sharing your faith. You are filled with his Holy Spirit and your heart and mind know his gospel. Within you, waiting to be activated by the Holy Spirit, are words that will bring life to people. One word of his, spoken by you, is enough to set someone free from the bondage of sin and death. Your potential is terrifying to the devil. He will do anything to keep you from sharing your faith. He will tell you that it's just for the evangelist. Don't listen! We must all do the work of an evangelist. Yes, some are called and anointed with the Holy Spirit to preach the gospel, but we are all called to share the gospel with others.

The gospel of Mark says that the last thing our Lord said to his followers, before ascending into heaven, was: 'Go everywhere in the world, and tell the Good News to everyone.' We are more than called – we are 'commanded' to go. You don't need to pray and ask God if he wants you to tell somebody the good news – just do it. Pray for opportunities and for doors to open, but just tell somebody, share your faith, develop friendships, be generous, give to your neighbours, buy lunch, smile and shake hands, be a listener to people's problems – whatever it takes for you to share your faith.

Time is running out for this generation, and we, the body of Christ, have been commanded to tell everyone the good news. We need God's wisdom to teach us to be skilful 'fishermen of men' as the Bible puts it. When you fish in the ocean you throw out big nets and try to draw as many fish in as possible. In the same way, when working with your church outreach team, try anything to win some lives. Throw out the big nets: hold concerts, carol services, street outreaches, plays, social nights, barbeques – whatever it takes. When fishing in the lake, take more care with your fish, don't just jump in and scare them away; be patient, take your time and skilfully reel in your catch. This is how it

let the love of Christ shine from you

should be with your family, friends and work colleagues. Take your time, let them feel at ease in your company, be warm and encouraging, let the love of Christ shine from you. Don't pull the Bible out in every conversation. God wants you to win the person over, not the argument. However, do not become complacent. As the Bible says, 'Show mercy to people who have doubts. Take others out of the fire, and save them' (Jude 22, 23).

You can be so caught up in the atmosphere of the world that when you do have a door opened to share your faith, those that have seen your lifestyle – your closest relatives, friends and family – will just think you are joking. Keep your eyes on Jesus, be comfortable with people and win them for Christ.

We have been commanded to tell the world the good news. It's the heartbeat of the Church. When the heart stops functioning, the body dies; when the body of Christ (the Church) stops sharing the good news, it dies. It doesn't matter how long the building has been standing or who the preacher is, the body must evangelise. We must tell the world this good news. And the good news for you is that he will do it through you. He will help. When your heart says, 'Yes Lord,' he will open the doors, he will open the conversations and he will give you the words to say. And he will build his body. Mark concludes his Gospel by saying, 'The followers went everywhere in the world and told the Good News to people, and the Lord helped them' (Mark 16:20). He helped them and he will help you. And unlike anything else you may achieve in this world – successful jobs, hobbies, relationships – it will make your spirit feel complete when you have been used by him to bring someone who was bound by darkness and imprisoned by sin, into your Father's arms. The vacuum is filled and the peace that passes all understanding enters your heart. The Bible says, 'I pray that the faith you share may make you understand every blessing we have in Christ' (Philemon verse 6).

As you give, you get back in abundance. Life for the members of Tough Talk was once all about self: gaining money, for some of us drinking ourselves to oblivion, for others it was about winning trophies – self, self, self! Now, life for us is about living to do what God wants, working to share our faith, going out and telling others the good news. This is what true life is all about. We know we are not perfect but, like all believers, we have this hope: that when Christ returns, we will be like him.

Author's Note: we, at Tough Talk, do not believe there is anything wrong with hobbies, jobs, relationships or even running a marathon! Just don't make these things idols. 'Be careful. Continue strong in the faith. Have courage, and be strong. Do everything in love' (1 Corinthians 16:13).

NOTES FOR GROWTH

1   We, the body of Christ, are witnesses of his life, death and
    resurrection.
    Your personal story of how you
    came to faith, is confirmation of
    his life, in your life.

2   Use your story as a way to share your faith with others. Be natural
    and try not to sound weird when telling your story.

3   Familiarise yourself with the Gospel of Jesus. The message of
    salvation is the heartbeat of the Church, be part of this amazing
    work of God.

4   'I pray that the faith you share may make you understand every
    blessing we have in Christ' (Philemon 6).

5   Dare to dream!

7 Proteins, Vitamins and Steroids

You must not have any other gods except me. . . .
You must not worship or serve any idol, because I,
the Lord your God, am a jealous God. . . .
You must not use the name of the Lord your God
thoughtlessly; the Lord will punish anyone who
misuses his name.
Remember to keep the Sabbath holy. . . .
Honour your father and your mother . . .
You must not murder anyone.
You must not be guilty of adultery.
You must not steal.
You must not tell lies about your neighbour.
You must not want to take your neighbour's house.
You must not want his wife or his male or female
slaves, or his ox or his donkey, or anything that
belongs to your neighbour.

Exodus 20:3–17

What a state of confusion I was in, standing in a local health food shop looking at all the protein powders and vitamins. What should I be taking? Do I need amino acids, liver tablets, multi-vitamins, extra vitamin B, whey protein, and milk and egg protein? Scratching my head I decided to read some magazines.

So I bought a couple of magazines, *Iron Man* and *Muscle and Fitness*. I wanted information and fast. Within hours I was sending off for more mags and books: *Ultimate Nutrition*, *Beef It*. The more I read the more confused I became. It seemed I needed to keep a constant nitrogen balance, and I needed carb drinks and protein shakes, multi-vitamins in the morning and minerals in the evening, protein bars, liver-drinks and everything else that was on the shelf. I even found myself taking kelp tablets. And cod liver oil capsules! My bedroom looked like a chemist. I remember my stepdad telling me, 'Ian, all you need is a good balanced diet.' 'Yeah,' I thought, 'and what do you know?' Then came the steroids. I spent eight years experimenting with every wonder drug that I could get my hands on. My body was like a pincushion.

A good balanced diet was all I needed

After ten years of wasting thousands of pounds and damaging my health (and buying out Holland and Barratt every week) I finally came to the conclusion that maybe my stepdad had been right all the time. A good balanced diet was all I needed. If only I had listened to that voice of wisdom all those years before. He had tried to explain that all the proteins, carbs, vitamins and minerals that I needed could be found in a good balanced diet, yet I had chosen to ignore him and go it alone and believe all the mags and supplement companies. What a waste of money and time.

As a Christian, I remember being in that same state of confusion. How should I act? Should I wear a suit? Should I try to talk all posh, grow my hair, become more religious looking? The only suit I had ever worn in my life was my door-suit for working on the doors of clubs. But I bought myself a suit and tried to become what I thought a Christian must be: a good person, helping others, smiling and shaking hands with strangers. Even if I was having a bad day, I didn't want anyone to know. I am a Christian; I must show everyone what a happy person I am. I was becoming kind of like Ned Flanders from *The Simpsons*. I was all over the place, trying to fit into this new world that I had found myself in. Then I thought, 'What about the Ten Commandments? That's what a Christian does, he keeps the Ten Commandments.' I had no idea even where to find them and I was too embarrassed to ask anyone. 'How embarrassing,' I thought. 'Everyone must know where they are and what they are all about.' So I spent three weeks reading from the beginning of the Bible, determined to locate these Christian commands. Then, bingo! Exodus 20, just as I was ready to give up.

Reading these commands from God I started to panic even more. I could get my head around the first five but nine and ten were going to be very difficult. Over the next few weeks and months I began my Christian project of trying to keep these rules. However, the more I tried not to lie, the more I seemed to be lying. The more I tried not to want what others had, the more I wanted.

I became very depressed and low. I got up one morning and just felt like lying flat on the floor face down. I couldn't do it; I couldn't be a Christian! I just wasn't a good person; the more I tried the harder it became. I wanted to bury my head in the ground and cry.

I got up, picked up my Bible and was about to put it away forever, but as I began to close the book, I noticed the title of the chapter 'Our Fight Against Sin' and I began to read. As I read, some of the words went over my head, but I read: 'But the law was the only way I could learn what sin meant. I would never have known what it means to want something wrong if the law had not said, "You must not want to take your neighbour's things." And sin found a way to use that command and cause me to want all kinds of things I should not want' (Romans 7:7–8).

'That's me,' I thought. My heart started to beat faster and I felt a rush all over. As I read further I found that it said the command was holy and good, but this struggle and pain was happening so I could see what sin was really like. Then I read, 'I want to do the things that are good, but I do not do them. I do not do the good things that I want to do, but I do the bad things that I do not want to do' (Romans 7:18–19). This was me! It was like being hit by a bolt.

> What I knew was that God was not condemning me, and through his Spirit was making me free

Then I read, 'What a miserable man I am!' (v. 24). This was everything I was going through and it was all in the Bible. It was as if Jesus was talking to me – and just me. This must have been written for a sinner like me. I had tried and failed; what a miserable man I was!

Then, like the sweet smell of the country air, like the moment you know everything's going to be alright, I read, 'Who will save me from this body that brings me death? I thank God for saving me through Jesus Christ our Lord!' (v. 24–25).

I didn't fully understand all that I was reading, but I knew Jesus knew what I was going through and he was going to rescue me. Then I read on in chapter 8, 'So now, those who are in Christ Jesus are not judged guilty. Through Christ Jesus the law of the Spirit that brings life made me free from the law that brings sin and death.' What a wonderful thing! What I knew was that God was not condemning me, and through his Spirit was making me free. I had discovered Romans Chapters 7 and 8. To compare it to discovering that I didn't need supplements or steroids to get strong is a cheap comparison – a bit like comparing a microwave dinner with a real home-made roast. No comparison. However, all that effort and pain was lifted in one moment. Jesus was not condemning but rescuing me. And the Commandments were there to show me what I was like.

I read and re-read Romans again and again. And I began to understand that the Commandments of God (also referred to as the Law) act like a mirror. When you look into a mirror you see the reflection of your face and any dirt or daily grime. In the same way, you look into the Laws of God and find you are a sinner, unable to keep your lips from gossip or lies, unable to stop yourself desiring what your neighbour has, loving yourself above anybody else, even God. The Bible says, 'There is no-one righteous not even one.'

When you see yourself in the mirror with dirt on your face, you go to the basin and wash your face clean. When you look into the Commandments and see you are unclean before a holy God, by faith you go to the basin full of the blood of Jesus and wash yourself clean.

What a revelation? In all my human effort I was unable to keep God's Laws. But as a Christian, as I followed Christ and lived by the Spirit, I found he would do it for me. I just needed to give him my struggles, my lies and gossip, and his Spirit would help me. Romans 8:13 says, 'But if you use the Spirit's help to stop doing the wrong things you do with your body, you will have true life.'

So now I wake up and offer myself to God and ask for his Spirit's help. (Romans 6:19 'In the same way now you must give yourselves to be slaves of goodness. Then you will live only for God.')

As a bodybuilder, I found all those supplements and steroids did very little for my bodybuilding. However, they did seriously damage my health. A balanced diet was all I needed. As a Christian, I found that all my efforts to be good and keep his Commandments failed. It was like hitting my head against a brick wall. But seeing Jesus and allowing him to work in me, offering myself to him on a daily basis – I knew that the Son of God had set me free.

NOTES FOR GROWTH:

★ **Be yourself**, don't try to act like someone else to prove you are a Christian. Allow God to deal with the real you – the inside.

★ His Spirit will give you the strength to do the right thing if you offer yourself daily to him.

★ Christianity is **24hrs-a-day** but by his love and Spirit he will enable you to overcome. You will always have bad days, but there's no judgement for those who are in Christ Jesus, his Spirit has **set us free**.

8 GOALS AND AIMS

'God knew them before he made the world, and he decided that they would be like his Son so that Jesus would be the firstborn of many brothers' (Romans 8:29).

Standing in front of the mirror, naked apart from a small pair of swimming trunks, I flexed and pumped my muscles, assessing my potential. Did I have what it takes to become a world champion? I knew I would never be satisfied with anything less. Could I make it to the top and raise the world title above my head?

Wag Bennett, the owner of the gym and a kind of guru in the bodybuilding world, was standing next to me. 'Lat spread from the front,' he would say. 'Side chest.' Wag encouraged me and told me that I had the potential to go all the way. To me this was the best news in the world.

As a young bodybuilder I always had a thirst for information and I was soon making plans, setting long- and short-term goals. I would write every detail in my diary, logging workouts, supplements and diets. I would set targets of how much weight I would need to be lifting at a certain time to give me the muscle increases I was after and build up my weak spots. I would study competitions, working out which ones I could compete in and win, who would be likely to turn up, what weight I would need to be entering in at. Then I would religiously work towards that goal, sacrificing everything to obtain the prize, fanatically weighing everything that went into my mouth, calculating carbs, proteins and fats. I knew the goal: one day I wanted to be the best in the world! I knew my short-term plans and objectives: how to eat and train, what courses I needed, what supplements to take. I was totally focused – religious to the core – training twice a day, seven days a week, no time for anything else. I would constantly fix my eyes on the goal, daily reassuring myself of the prize.

Becoming obsessed with the dream

For me, bodybuilding became a selfish obsession that nearly destroyed my life. I would have given up anything to become a world champion bodybuilder. I lost balance and became totally self-obsessed.

As a Christian reading the Bible, I noticed this was how motivated the early disciples were with their faith. But they weren't 'self-obsessed', they were 'Christ-obsessed'. Giving their lives to Christ really meant giving it all to him. They lived 100 per cent Christ-centred lives. They knew their destiny; it was all or nothing, moving constantly towards the goal. (Philippians 3:14 'I keep trying to reach the goal and get the prize for which God called me through Christ to the life above.') They were focused in their faith; they had aims and objectives; they were purpose driven, with zeal and enthusiasm. They lived following the master, pursuing holiness, preaching and teaching, worshipping and praying. It was more than attending church once a week. They had plans, and were getting ready for the master's return, always being led by the Holy Spirit, doing mighty exploits with God. It doesn't matter how long you have been a Christian, you need encouragement, balance and direction. You need to stay focused on Jesus, as he stayed focused on his goal. (Hebrews 12:2, 'He suffered death on the cross. But he accepted the shame as if it were nothing because of the joy that God put before him. And now he is sitting at the right side of God's throne.') Jesus was focused on his mission. Nothing was going to deter him or put him off course. On many occasions, attempts were made to take his eyes off the prize, to lead him away from the cross. 'From that time on Jesus began telling his followers that he must go to Jerusalem, where the older Jewish leaders, the leading priests, and the teachers of the law would make him suffer many things. He told them he must be killed and then be raised from the dead on the third day. Peter took Jesus aside and told him not to talk like that. He said, "God save you from those things, Lord! Those things will never happen to you!" Then Jesus said to Peter "Go away from me, Satan! You are not helping me! You don't care about the things of God, but only about the things people think are important"' (Matthew 16:21–23).

Whenever you set down your intentions, aims and ambitions, if they are what God wants, somebody's going to try and put you off your goal. 'You can't write a book!' 'You, lead someone to Christ? Yeah right!' 'You, have a singing ministry? I'd like to see that!' And be careful, because it could come from those that are closest to you.

Jesus knew that Peter was not talking with the things of God in his mind, and dealt sharply with it, cutting Peter's pleasant-sounding words of comfort dead. I am not advising you to tell your loved ones to 'get out of my sight, Satan!' However, you may have to stop their opposition to what God has planned for you, right there and then, without letting it affect your thinking negatively. 'Thank you very much for you advice, but I am going to sing for God anyway.' 'Your words are encouraging, however I intend to complete what God has called me to do.'

know what God has called you to do and stick to it

Later, as the time was getting closer for Jesus to go to the cross and his popularity was overpowering his aims, again and again he had to keep focused. One such time was after the triumphal entry into Jerusalem, when crowds had gathered and sung 'Praise God!' 'God bless the one who comes in the name of the Lord!' 'God bless the King of Israel!' (John 12:13.) The people were proclaiming him King of Israel and this was a serious statement. Even his enemies were saying, 'Look! The whole world is following him!' (John 12:19).

Jesus needed to keep his eye on the goal, knowing what God had called him to do. Often when you are doing just what God has called you to do, something comes along that seems like it's from God, but it may pull you off course. Jesus had come to be a king, for he is the King of Kings and Lord of Lords. Yet God didn't want him to set up an earthly kingdom, in the way the people saw it. First he had to be the 'suffering servant', the 'sacrificial lamb'. He had to die and rise again.

If God has called you to be an evangelist, don't suddenly accept that pastoral job. Yes, it may give you a regular income, but know what God has called you to do and stick to it, reach your goal in Christ. Fulfil your calling in him.

John 12:20 tells us of some Greeks who came to see Jesus – people of position and power. How excited the disciples must have been at this time. What a wonderful day; the people had been calling their master 'King of Israel' and now the Greeks had come to see Jesus. Wow! Jesus, their master, looked like he would become King and restore the Kingdom of Israel.

Knowing his popularity was at boiling point, Jesus reminded himself and his disciples of the goal in front of him: 'Jesus said to them, "The time has come for the Son of Man to receive his glory. I tell you the truth, a grain of wheat must fall to the ground and die to make many seeds. But if it never dies, it remains only a single seed"' (John 12:23–24). Jesus was not prepared to let popularity or difficult circumstances or any other situation put him off course. Jesus then concludes this statement with a message for those who follow him: 'Those who love their lives will lose them, but those who hate their lives in this world will keep true life for ever. Whoever serves me must follow me. Then my servant will be with me wherever I am' (John 12:25).

Strong words, but 100 per cent commitment is required. You must start by giving your whole life and then you will despise your old ways of seeking self-gains and pleasure. Your life is now lived for Christ.

Eventually we who serve him must follow him to his cross. We need to make him Lord of our lives and live in obedience to the

Holy Spirit. Then we will keep our lives for eternity. Your goal is in him; your focus is in serving him; your life becomes Christ-centred. You are now part of the body of Christ. Allow him to build you and use you as a functioning part of that body. And as you develop your faith and build up your spiritual body and stay attached to the head that is Christ, he will take you on a journey of faith, a journey of valleys and mountains, of giant-slaying and mountain-moving. Keep your eyes focused on him, and pursue him with all your body and soul.

The end product

The final stage of competitive bodybuilding is being victorious.

Whatever we do in life, at the end we want to know we have done our best, given it our all and made a difference. For a Christian, one day we will stand before our God and he will welcome us into his kingdom, and those that lived the life and followed his way will hear him say, 'well done my good and faithful servant'. And so we will be with God forever.

What a wonderful thought – a life of hope, destiny and purpose. The gospel is a cause worth living for. Jesus is the way, the truth and the life and no one can come to the Father except through him. He is our eternal destiny. And to achieve this you accept him by faith, and by faith you walk with him. The path is narrow and only a few find it, but with him we can stay on that narrow road which leads to eternity with him.

I have always hated 1-to-10 lists on how to do anything when it comes serving God. However, I have listed a reminder and a guide to what you need to do as you live your life for God:

1. Find a church (you need other Christians).

2. Begin to pray (this is your relationship with your heavenly Father).

3. Read your Bible (it will provide nourishment for your spirit).

4. Tell people (share your faith, give your story).

5. Ask for help when you are struggling.

6. Get baptised. (This for when you feel ready. Baptism is your declaration of commitment to Jesus. It symbolises leaving your old life behind as you come up from the water. Talk to a church leader about this.)

7. Keep it real (let Christ change the inside, don't try to fabricate this by acting like somebody else).

8. Memorise God's word (you will do well to learn Scripture, it will guide your life).

9. Think of others (be a light in this generation, care for others).

10. "'You must do these things to enjoy life and have many happy days. You must not say evil things, and you must not tell lies. Stop doing evil and do good. Look for peace and work for it. The Lord sees good people and listens to their prayers. But the Lord is against those who do evil.'" (1 Peter 3:10–12 and Psalm 34:12–16).

In conclusion, I want to encourage you to go for it and not to look back: 'As you received Christ Jesus the Lord, so continue to live in him. Keep your roots deep in him and have your lives built on him. Be strong in the faith, just as you were taught, and always be thankful' (Colossians 2:6–7). You are part of the body of Christ and every part is important. An eye cannot say it has no need for the hand; every member of his body has a function. So be strong in your faith and be led in the calling of your life.

'Be an example to the believers with your words, your actions, your love, your faith, and your pure life' (1 Timothy 4:12).